Garter Stitch
For Baby

Garter Stitch is not only one of the easiest stitches to master—just knit every row—
but it also has a wonderful texture that will enhance any project. All of the projects in
this book will be a joy to knit, whether you pick a blanket, sweater, booties or hat.

LEISURE ARTS, INC. • Little Rock, Arkansas

Baby Hat

SHOPPING LIST

Yarn Worsted Weight **4** yarn, 100% acrylic, 3½ oz/100g, (approx 175 yds/156m)

☐ Color A: 1 Skein Off White
☐ Color B: 1 Skein Green

Knitting Needles

☐ US 9 (5.5 mm) or size needed for gauge
☐ US 8 (5 mm)
☐ US 7 (4.5 mm)

Additional Supplies

☐ Yarn needle

SIZE INFORMATION

Size: 3-6 months (12, 18 months)
Head circumference: 14 (15, 16)" / 35.5 (38, 40.5) cm

GAUGE INFORMATION

13 sts and 24 rows per 4" / 10 cm in Garter Stitch using size US 9 (5.5 mm) needles.

Hat

Using A and size US 9 (5.5 mm) needles, cast on 48 (50, 52) sts. Work in Garter Stitch (knit every row) until piece measures 4" / 10 cm.

Change to B and work until piece measures 5½" / 14 cm.

Change to size US 8 (5 mm) needles and work until piece measures 6¾" / 17 cm.

Change to size US 7 (4.5 mm) needles and work until piece measures 8" / 20.5 cm

Next row: K2tog to end of row – 24 (25, 26) sts.

Next row: K0 (1, 0), k2tog to end of row – 12 (13, 13) sts.

Next row: While binding off, k0 (1, 1), k2tog to end.

FINISHING

Sew seam. Draw yarn through bound off row, pull tight and fasten off. Weave in ends.

Leg Warmers

SHOPPING LIST

Yarn Worsted Weight  yarn, 100% acrylic, 3½ oz/100g, (approx 197 yds / 180m)

- ☐ Color A: 1 Skein Off White
- ☐ Color B: 1Skein Green
- ☐ Color C: 1 Skein Pink

Knitting Needles

- ☐ US 9 (5.5 mm) or size needed for gauge
- ☐ US 7 (4.5 mm)

Additional Supplies

- ☐ Yarn needle

SIZE INFORMATION

Size: One Size

GAUGE INFORMATION

13 sts and 24 rows per 4" / 10 cm in Garter Stitch using size US 9 (5.5 mm) needles.

Stripe Pattern

4 rows Off White

2 rows Green

4 rows Off White

2 rows Pink

Leg Warmer

Make 2

With Off White and smaller needles cast on 22 sts and knit 5 rows.
Knit 1 kfb, knit 8, kfb, knit 9 – 24 sts.

Change to larger needles and keeping in Garter Stitch (knit every row), begin Stripe Pattern with Green.

Work until piece measures approx. 7" and ready for an Off White row. Change to Off White and smaller needles and knit 1, k2 tog, knit 9, k2 tog, knit 10.

Work 5 more rows, bind off.

FINISHING

Sew seam.

Ripple Stripe Blanket

■■□□ **EASY**

SIZE INFORMATION

Size: 27" (68.5 cm) wide x
36" (91.5 cm) long

GAUGE INFORMATION

16 sts and 20 rows per 4" / 10 cm
in Ripple Stripe Pattern

Ripple Stripe Pattern – multiple
of 18 sts

Row 1 (RS): * [K2tog] 3 times,
[k1, yo] 6 times, [k2tog] 3 times;
repeat from * to end.

Rows 2, 3 and 4: Knit.

Repeat these 4 rows for pattern.

Blanket

Using A, cast on 108 sts.
Work in Ripple Stripe Pattern,
changing colors in the following
sequence:

20 rows with A.

20 rows with B.

20 rows with A.

20 rows with C.

20 rows with A.

20 rows with D.

20 rows with A.

20 rows with E.

20 rows with A.

Bind off.

FINISHING

Weave in ends.

Ripple Stripe Pattern

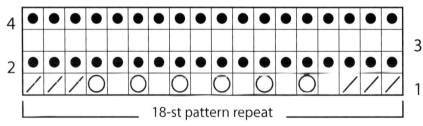

18-st pattern repeat

☐ k on RS, p on WS   ○ yo

● p on RS, k on WS   ╱ k2tog

Teal Stripe Blanket

■■□□ **EASY**

SHOPPING LIST

Yarn Worsted Weight
yarn, 100% acrylic, 3½ oz/100g
(approx 205 yds/187m)

- ☐ Color A: 2 Skeins White
- ☐ Color B: 1 Skein Light Teal
- ☐ Color C: 1 Skein Dark Teal

Knitting Needles

- ☐ US 13 (9 mm) or size needed
  for gauge

Additional Supplies

- ☐ Yarn needle

SIZE INFORMATION

Size: 28 ½" (72 cm) wide x 30"
(81 cm) long

GAUGE INFORMATION

11 sts and 10 rows per 4" / 10 cm
in Garter Stitch (knit every row)
with 2 strands of yarn held
together.

Note: The blanket is worked in 3
panels, each 9½" wide by 30" long.

Note: The blanket is worked with
2 strands of yarn held together
throughout.

Panel 1 (Make 2)

With White, cast on 28 sts and
working in Garter Stitch (knit
every row), begin Stripe Pattern
as follows:

**Rows 1, 2, 5, 6, 9, 10, 13, 14, 17,
18, 21, 22:** knit with White.

**Rows 3, 4, 7, 8, 11, 12, 15, 16, 19,
20:** knit with Light Teal.

**Rows 23, 24, 27, 28, 31, 32, 35,
36, 39, 40, 43, 44, 47, 48, 51, 52:**
knit with Dark Teal.

**Rows 25, 26, 29, 30, 33, 34, 37,
38, 41, 42, 45, 46, 49, 50:** knit
with White.

**Rows 53, 54, 57, 58, 61, 62, 65,
66, 69, 70:** knit with Light Teal.

**Rows 55, 56, 59, 60, 63, 64, 67,
68, 71, 72:** knit with Dark Teal.
Bind off all sts.

Panel 2

With Dark Teal, cast on 28 sts and
working in Garter Stitch, begin
Stripe Pattern as follows:

**Rows 1, 2, 5, 6, 9, 10, 13, 14, 17, 18,
21, 22:** knit with Dark Teal.

**Rows 3, 4, 7, 8, 11, 12, 15, 16, 19,
20, 23, 24:** knit with Light Teal.

**Rows 25, 26, 29, 30, 33, 34, 37, 38,
41, 42, 45, 46, 49, 50, 53, 54:** knit
with White.

**Rows 27, 28, 31, 32, 35, 36, 39, 40,
43, 44, 47, 48, 51, 52:** knit with
Light Teal.

**Rows 55, 56, 59, 60, 63, 64, 67, 68,
71, 72:** knit with Dark Teal.

Rows 57, 58, 61, 62, 65, 66, 69, 70:
knit with White. Bind off.

FINISHING

Sew panels together, with Panel
2 between the two Panel 1's.

Hooded Sweater

Designed by Lee Gant

■■■□ INTERMEDIATE

SIZE INFORMATION

Size: 6 (12, 18, 24) months
Chest: 20 (22, 24, 26)" / 51 (56, 61, 66) cm
Length: 11 (12, 13, 14)" / 28 (30.5, 33, 35.5) cm

GAUGE INFORMATION

16 sts and 32 rows per 4" / 10 cm in Garter Stitch

Coat
Body

Cast on 88 (96, 104, 112) sts.
Row 1 (WS): K27 (29, 31, 33), p1, k40 (44, 48, 52), p1, k19 (21, 23, 25).
Row 2 (RS): Knit.
Repeat these 2 rows until piece measures 5 (5½, 5½, 6)" / 12.5 (14, 14, 15) cm, ending with a WS row.
Next row – Buttonhole Row (RS): Knit to last 5 sts, k2tog, yo twice, k2tog, k1.
Next row (WS): K3, p1, k23 (25, 27, 29), p1, k40 (44, 48, 52), p1, k19 (21, 23, 25).
Continue in established pattern (Rows 1 and 2) until piece measures 7 (7½, 7½, 8)" / 18 (19, 19, 20.5) cm, ending with a WS row.
Next row (RS): Repeat Buttonhole Row.
Next row (WS): K3, p1, k23 (25, 27, 29), p1, k40 (44, 48, 52), p1, k19 (21, 23, 25).

Divide for Front and Back

Next row (RS): K16 (18, 20, 22), BO 7, k34 (38, 40, 46), BO 7, knit to end.
Continue on 24 (26, 28, 30) Left Front sts only. Place Right Front and Back sts on holder.

Left Front

Row 1 (WS): Knit.
Row 2 (RS): K2tog, knit to end – 23 (25, 27, 29) sts.
Rows 3 and 4: Repeat Rows 1 and 2 – 22 (24, 26, 28) sts.
Work even in Garter Stitch (knit every row) until piece measures 9 (9½, 9½, 10)" / 23 (24, 24, 25.5) cm, ending with a WS row.
Next row – Buttonhole Row (RS): Knit to last 5 sts, k2tog, yo twice, k2tog, k1.
Next row (WS): K3, p1, knit to end. Knit 3 rows.

Shape Neck

Row 1 (WS): BO 9, knit to end – 13 (15, 17, 19) sts.
Row 2 (RS): Knit.
Row 3: BO 3, knit to end – 10 (12, 14, 16) sts.
Row 4: Knit.
Row 5: BO 3, knit to end – 7 (9, 11, 13) sts.
Work even in Garter Stitch until piece measures 11 (12, 13, 14)" / 28 (30.5, 33, 35.5) cm from beginning. Place sts on holder.

Continued on page 12.

Right Front

Rejoin yarn to Right Front sts at armhole edge – 16 (18, 20, 22) sts.

Row 1 (WS): K2tog, knit to end – 15 (17, 19, 21) sts.

Row 2 (RS): Knit.

Rows 3 and 4: Repeat Rows 1 and 2 – 14 (16, 18, 20) sts.

Work even in Garter Stitch until same length as Left Front to neck shaping, ending with a WS row.

Shape Neck

Row 1 (RS): BO 4, knit to end – 10 (12, 14, 16) sts.

Row 2 (WS): Knit.

Row 3: BO 3, knit to end – 7 (9, 11, 13) sts.

Work even in Garter Stitch until piece measures 11 (12, 13, 14)" / 28 (30.5, 33, 35.5) cm from beginning. Place sts on holder.

Back

Rejoin yarn to Back sts at left armhole edge – 34 (38, 42, 46) sts.

Row 1 (WS): K2tog, knit to last 2 sts, k2tog – 32 (36, 40, 44) sts.

Row 2 (RS): Knit.

Row 3: Repeat Row 1 – 30 (34, 38, 42) sts.

Work even in Garter Stitch until piece measures 11 (12, 13, 14)" / 28 (30.5, 33, 35.5) cm from beginning. Place 7 (9, 11, 13) sts for each shoulder on holders. Place center 16 sts on another holder for back neck.

Sleeves

Cast on 24 (26, 28, 30) sts.

Work 9 rows in Garter Stitch.

Next row – Increase Row (RS): Kfb, knit to last st, kfb – 26 (28, 30, 32) sts.

Continuing in Garter Stitch, repeat Increase Row every 10th row 3 (3, 3, 4) more times – 32 (34, 36, 40) sts.

Work even in Garter Stitch until piece measures 6½ (7, 7½, 8)" / 16.5 (18, 19, 20.5) cm, ending with a WS row.

Shape Cap

Rows 1 and 2: BO 3, knit to end – 26 (28, 30, 34) sts.

Row 3: K2tog, knit to last 2 sts, k2tog – 24 (26, 28, 32) sts.

Row 4: Knit.

Row 5: K2tog, knit to last 2 sts, k2tog – 22 (24, 26, 30) sts.

Knit 2 (2, 3, 3) rows.

Next row: K2tog, knit to last 2 sts, k2tog – 20 (22, 24, 28) sts.

Knit 3 (3, 3, 4) rows.

Next row: K2tog, knit to last 2 sts, k2tog – 18 (20, 22, 26) sts.

Knit 4 rows.

Next 2 rows: BO 4 (4, 4, 5), knit to end – 10 (12, 14, 16) sts.

Next 2 rows: BO 3 (3, 4, 4), knit to end – 4 (6, 6, 8) sts.

Bind off.

FINISHING

Join shoulder seams using 3-Needle Bind-Off *(Fig. 1, page 28)*. Sew sleeve seams. Sew sleeves into armholes.

Hood

Starting at Right Front neck edge, with RS facing, pick up and knit 8 (8, 10, 12) sts along Right Front neck edge, kfb in each stitch from holder at back neck, then pick up and knit 16 (16, 18, 20) sts along Left Front neck edge – 56 (56, 60, 64) sts.

Work in Garter Stitch until hood measures 3 (3, 4, 4)" / 7.5 (7.5, 10, 10) cm from neck edge, ending with a RS row.

Next row (WS): K19 (19, 20, 21), pm, k18 (18, 20, 22), pm, knit to end.

Next row (RS): * Knit to 3 sts before marker, k2tog, k1, slip marker, k1, k2tog; repeat from * once, knit to end – 52 (52, 56, 60) sts.
Knit 4 rows.

Next row: * Knit to 3 sts before marker, k2tog, k1, slip marker, k1, k2tog; repeat from * once, knit to end – 48 (48, 52, 56) sts.
Knit 4 rows.

Next row: * Knit to 3 sts before marker, k2tog, k1, slip marker, k1, k2tog; repeat from * once, knit to end – 44 (44, 48, 52) sts.
Work even in Garter Stitch until hood measures 5½ (6, 6½ 7)" / 14 (15, 16.5, 18) cm from neck edge. Divide sts onto 2 needles and join

at top of hood using 3-Needle Bind-Off with WS facing.
Using crochet hook, work 1 round of Crochet Slip Stitch *(Fig. 5, page 29)* around outer edge of jacket, hood and sleeve cuffs. Sew decorative buttons to left front 1½" / 4 cm away from buttonholes. Sew functional buttons to right front to correspond to buttonholes. Weave in ends.

Schematic Diagram

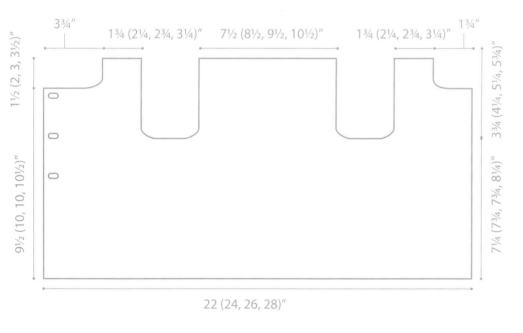

Vest

Designed by Bonnie Reardon

SHOPPING LIST

Yarn Worsted Weight yarn, 100% acrylic, 7 oz/198g, (approx 364 yds/125m)

☐ Color A: 1 Skein Light Blue
☐ Color B: 1 Skein Windsor Blue

Knitting Needles

☐ 16" circular US 8 (5 mm) or size needed for gauge
☐ Set of 4 double pointed needles
☐ US 8 (5 mm)

Additional Supplies

☐ Stitch marker
☐ Stitch holders
☐ Yarn needle

SIZE INFORMATION

Size: 12 months (2, 4, 6 years)
Chest: 20 (22, 25½, 27½)" / 51 (56, 65, 70) cm
Length: 11 (12, 13, 14)" / 28 (30.5, 33, 35.5) cm

GAUGE INFORMATION

14 ½ sts and 27 rows per 4" / 10 cm in Garter Stitch

SPECIAL TECHNIQUE: Garter Stitch in the Round

This technique allows you to knit Garter Stitch in the round without purling every other round. Knit to the end of the round. *Slip marker, slip next st. Bring yarn to front. Turn work. Slip first st, slip marker. Knit to end of round. Repeat from * for each round. This creates a wrapped stitch when the work is turned. The wraps blend in to the Garter Stitch; there is no need to knit the wrap together with the wrapped stitch.

Vest
Body

Using circular needle and A, cast on 72 (80, 92, 100) sts. Place marker for beginning of round and join to work in the round, being careful not to twist stitches. Using Garter Stitch in the Round Technique, knit 6 rounds with A.
Knit 8 rounds with B.
Knit 6 rounds with A.
Knit 6 rounds with B.
Knit 4 rounds with A.

Knit 4 rounds with B.
Knit 2 rounds with A.
Knit 2 rounds with B.
Knit with A until piece measures 7 (7½, 8, 8½)" / 18 (19, 20.5, 21.5) cm, ending with a WS round.

Divide for Front and Back

Next round (RS): BO 4, k28 (32, 38, 42) sts, BO 8, k28 (32, 38, 42) sts, BO 4. Break yarn and fasten off.

Back

Rejoin yarn to last group of 28 (32, 38, 42) sts worked. Place remaining 28 (32, 38, 42) sts on holder for Front.
Row 1 (WS): Knit.
Row 2 (RS): K1, ssk, knit to last 3 sts, k2tog, k1.
Repeat last 2 rows once more – 24 (28, 34, 38) sts.
Work even in Garter Stitch until piece measures 11 (12, 13, 14)" / 28 (30.5, 33, 35.5) cm from beginning, ending with a WS row. Place sts on holder.

Continued on page 16.

Continued on page 16.

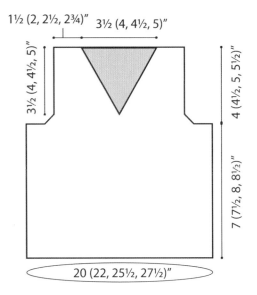

1½ (2, 2½, 2¾)"   3½ (4, 4½, 5)"

3½ (4, 4½, 5)"

4 (4½, 5, 5½)"

7 (7½, 8, 8½)"

20 (22, 25½, 27½)"

Front

Rejoin yarn to Front sts at right armhole edge.

Row 1 (WS): Knit.

Row 2 (RS): K1, ssk, knit to last 3 sts, k2tog, k1.

Repeat last 2 rows once more – 24 (28, 34, 38) sts.

Row 5 (WS): Knit.

Row 6 (RS): K9 (11, 14, 16), k2tog, k1, turn work. Place remaining 12 (14, 17, 19) sts on holder for Right Front. Continue on Left Front only.

Row 7 and all wrong side rows: Knit.

Row 8: Knit to last 3 sts, k2tog, k1 – 1 st decreased.

Repeat last two rows 4 (5, 6, 7) more times – 6 (7, 8, 9) sts. Work even in Garter Stitch until same length as back to shoulder. Place on holder.

Rejoin yarn to Right Front sts at neck edge.

Row 1 (RS): K1, ssk, knit to end – 11 (13, 16, 18) sts.

Row 2 and all wrong side rows: Knit.

Repeat these 2 rows 5 (6, 7, 8) more times – 6 (7, 9, 10) sts. Work even in Garter Stitch until same length as back to shoulder.

FINISHING

Join shoulder seams using 3-Needle Bind-Off (**Fig. 1, page 28**).

Neckband

Place remaining 12 (14, 16, 18) sts from back neck on dpn. Join B at right shoulder seam and knit back neck sts. With a second dpn, pick up and knit 3 sts for every 4 rows down left front neck edge and 1 st at the center of the V neck. With a third dpn, pick up and knit 3 sts for every 4 rows up right front neck edge. Place marker and join to work in the round.

Round 1: Slip one st, bring yarn to front, turn work. Slip 1 st, slip marker, knit to end of round. Continue using Garter Stitch in the Round Technique.

Round 2 (RS): Knit to 1 st before center of V neck, k3tog, knit to end of round.

Round 3: Knit.

Bind off.

Armbands

Join B to bound off sts at armhole. Using dpns, pick up and knit 1 st for every bound off stitch at bottom of armhole, then 3 sts for every 4 rows along front and back armhole edges. Place marker and join to work in the round.

Knit 3 rounds using Garter Stitch in the Round Technique. Bind off. Weave in ends.

Sweetie Toy

Designed by Wendy Rolonstein

SHOPPING LIST

Yarn Worsted Weight yarn, 100% acrylic, 3½ oz/100g, (approx 170 yds/156m)

- ☐ Color A: 1 Skein Taupe
- ☐ Color B: 1 Skein Beige
- ☐ Color C: 1 Skein Dusty Rose

Knitting Needles

- ☐ US 8 (5 mm) or size needed for gauge
- ☐ 2 Double pointed needles US 8 (5 mm)

Additional Supplies

- ☐ Stitch holders
- ☐ Yarn needle
- ☐ Fiberfill stuffing

SIZE INFORMATION

Size: 10" (25.5 cm) tall

GAUGE INFORMATION:

16 sts and 32 rows per 4" / 10 cm in Garter Stitch

Doll
Body Back

Using A, cast on 20 sts.
Knit 15 rows.
Row 16 (RS): K1, m1, k18, m1, k1 – 22 sts.
Row 17 (WS): Knit.
Row 18: K1, m1, k20, m1, k1 – 24 sts.
Row 19: Knit.
Row 20: K1, m1, k22, m1, k1 – 26 sts.
Rows 21-25: Knit 15 rows.
Row 36: K12 and put on holder for left leg, BO2, k12.

Right Leg Back

Row 1 (WS): K10, k2tog – 11 sts.
Row 2 (RS): K9, k2tog – 10 sts.
Row 3: K8, k2tog – 9 sts.
Row 4: K7, k2tog – 8 sts.
Row 5: K6, k2tog – 7 sts.
Row 6: K5, k2tog – 6 sts.
Bind off.

Left Leg Back

Rejoin yarn to Left Leg sts at inseam.
Work Rows 1-6 same as for Right Leg Back.
Bind off.

Body Front

Using B, cast on 20 sts.
Knit 15 rows.
Change to A.
Row 16 (RS): K1, m1, k18, m1, k1 – 22 sts.
Row 17 (WS): Knit.
Row 18: K1, m1, k20, m1, k1 – 24 sts.
Row 19: Knit.
Row 20: K1, m1, k22, m1, k1 – 26 sts.
Rows 21-25: Knit 15 rows.
Row 36: K12 and put on holder for right leg, BO2, k12.

Left Leg Front

Row 1 (WS): K10, k2tog – 11 sts.
Row 2 (RS): K9, k2tog – 10 sts.
Row 3: K8, k2tog – 9 sts.
Row 4: K7, k2tog – 8 sts.
Change to C.
Row 5: K6, k2tog – 7 sts.
Row 6: K5, k2tog – 6 sts.
Bind off.

Continued on next page.

Right Leg Front

Rejoin yarn to Right Leg sts at inseam.

Work Rows 1-6 same as for Left Leg Front.

Bind off.

Arms (make 2)

With B, cast on 20 sts.

Rows 1 and 2: Knit.

Row 3: Ssk, knit to last 2 sts, k2tog – 18 sts.

Rows 4 and 5: Knit.

Row 6: Ssk, knit to last 2 sts, k2tog – 16 sts.

Rows 7 and 8: Knit.

Row 9: Ssk, knit to last 2 sts, k2tog – 14 sts.

Rows 10 and 11: Knit.

Change to C.

Row 12: Ssk, knit to last 2 sts, k2tog – 12 sts.

Rows 13 and 14: Knit.

Row 15: Ssk, knit to last 2 sts, k2tog – 10 sts.

Rows 16 and 17: Knit.

Row 18: Ssk, knit to last 2 sts, k2tog – 8 sts.

Row 19: Knit.

Bind off.

Head (Make 2)

With B, cast on 20 sts.

Knit 6 rows.

Row 7 (RS): K1, m1, k18, m1, k1 – 22 sts.

Rows 8 and 9: Knit.

Row 10 (WS): K1, m1, k20, m1, k1 – 24 sts.

Row 11: Knit.

Change to A.

Row 12: Knit.

Change to B.

Rows 13-26: Knit 14 rows.

Bind off.

FINISHING

Weave in ends.

Sew back and front of body and legs together, leaving top open. Stuff.

Sew heads together, leaving neck open. Stuff.

Sew head to body.

Fold arms in half and sew seam. Stuff.

Sew arms to body.

Tie

With dpns and C, cast on 4 sts.

* Do not turn work. Bring yarn behind sts and k4. Repeat from * until cord is 30" (76 cm) long.

Bind off.

Sew center of cord to center back neck. Tie cord around neck in a bow.

Face Embroidery

Working on Front Head only with C, work Satin Stitch *(Fig. 2, page 29)* at head corners for ears. With C, work mouth in Backstitch *(Fig. 3, page 29)*. With A, work eyes in Backstitch.

Booties

SHOPPING LIST

Yarn Worsted Weight  yarn, 100% acrylic, 3½ oz /100g (approx 200 yds / 182m)

☐ 1 Skein Multicolor Pink and Green

Knitting Needles

☐ US 7 (4.5 mm) or size needed for gauge

Additional Supplies

☐ Yarn needle

SIZE INFORMATION

Size: 3-6 months

GAUGE INFORMATION:

17 sts and 32 rows per 4" / 10 cm in Garter Stitch using size US 7 (4.5 mm) needles.

Sole

Cast on 26 sts.

Row 1 (RS): Knit.

Row 2 (WS): K1, yo, k11, [yo, k1] twice, yo, k11, yo, k1 – 31 sts.

Rows 3, 5, 7 and 9: Knit, working each yarn over through the back loop.

Row 4: K2, yo, k11, yo, k2, yo, k3, yo, k11, yo, k2 – 36 sts.

Row 6: K3, yo, k11, [yo, k4] twice, yo, k11, yo, k3 – 41 sts.

Row 8: Knit.

Sides

Starting with a RS row, knit 4 rows.

Instep

Row 1 (RS): K23, ssk, turn work. 16 sts remain unworked.

Row 2 (WS): Sl 1, k5, k2tog, turn work.

Row 3: Sl 1, k5, ssk, turn work.

Rows 4-12: Repeat Rows 2 and 3 four more times, then work Row 2 once more – 29 sts.

Row 13 (RS): Sl 1, k5, ssk, knit to end of row.

Row 14: K16, k2tog, purl to end of row – 27 sts.

Cuff

Knit 11 rows. Bind off.

FINISHING

Sew sole seam and center back seam.

Mitts

 **EASY**

SIZE INFORMATION

Size: One size
Length: 4"

GAUGE

16 sts and 32 rows per 4"/10 cm in Garter Stitch using a single strand of yarn

K1 P1 Rib:

Worked over an odd number of stitches:

Row 1 (RS): P1, * k1, p1; repeat from * to end.
Row 2 (WS): K1, * p1, k1; repeat from * to end.

Garter Stitch:

Knit every row.

Notes: While working stripes, do not cut the yarn when changing colors. Carry the yarn not in use loosely up the side of the piece.

Cuff

Cast on 24 sts.
Work 7 rows K1 P1 Rib.

Hand

Work 20 rows in Garter Stitch.

Shape Tip

Row 1 (RS): * K2tog, k1; repeat from * to end – 16 sts.
Row 2 and all WS rows: Knit.
Row 3: K1, * k2tog, k1; repeat from * to end – 11 sts.
Row 5: K1, * k2tog; repeat from * to end – 6 sts.
Bind off.

Repeat for other hand.

FINISHING

Sew side and tip seams.

Cord

Using crochet hook, make chain 14" long. Attach one end of cord to each mitt.

VARIATIONS

Green Tipped Mitts

Use Ivory for cuff and first 14 rows of Garter Stitch. Change to Green for remainder of mitt. Use Ivory for cord.

Blue Striped Mitts

Cast on and work first row of rib with Blue. Work 6 rows of rib with Ivory. For Garter Stitch, alternate 4 rows of Ivory with 2 rows of Blue. Use Blue for cord.

Fingerless Mitts

SHOPPING LIST

Yarn Worsted Weight 4 MEDIUM

100% acrylic, 3½ oz/100g (approx. 175 yds/156m)

- ☐ Color A: 1 Skein Pink; approx. 10 yds
- ☐ Color B: 1 Skein Ivory; approx. 25 yds

Knitting Needles

- ☐ US 7 (4.5 mm) or size needed to obtain gauge

Additional Supplies

- ☐ Yarn needle

SIZE INFORMATION

Size: One size

Length: 3½"

GAUGE

16 sts and 24 rows = per 4"/10 cm in Stockinette st

K1 P1 Rib:

Worked over an odd number of stitches:

Row 1 (RS): P1, * k1, p1; repeat from * to end.

Row 2 (WS): K1, * p1, k1; repeat from to end.

Cuff

With color A, cast on 25 sts.

Work 1 row K1 P1 Rib.

Change to color B.

Work 5 rows K1 P1 Rib.

Change to Stockinette st and work even until piece measures 3". Change to color A and knit 2 rows. Bind off.

FINISHING Embroidery

Use color A to work zig-zag chart in Duplicate Stitch *(Figs. 4a-b, page 29)* around cuff. Position bottom row of chart on Row 2 of Stockinette st.

Sew side seam from cast-on edge to top of ribbing. Leave 1" open for thumb hole. Sew remainder of side seam to bound-off edge.

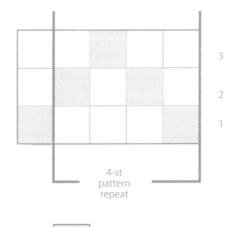

4-st pattern repeat

duplicate stitch with color A

General Instructions

ABBREVIATIONS

BO	Bind Off
ch	chain
CO	Cast on
dpn(s)	double pointed needle(s)
k	knit
kfb	knit in the front and the back of the next stitch
k2tog	knit 2 stitches together
k3tog	knit 2 stitches together
m1	make 1 stitch: Insert left needle, from front to back, under strand of yarn which runs between next stitch on left needle and last stitch on right needle; knit this stitch through back loop. 1 stitch Increased.
p	purl
p2tog	purl 2 stitches together
pm	place marker on needle
RS	Right Side
sc	single crochet
sl	slip next stitch as if to purl
ssk	slip, slip, knit – slip 2 stitches separately as if to knit, slip them together back to the left needle, then knit them together through the back loops
st(s)	stitch(es)
St st	Stockinette stitch – knit the right side rows, purl the wrong side rows
WS	Wrong Side
yo	yarn over

3-NEEDLE BIND-OFF

Place the stitches to be joined on two needles. Hold needles parallel with RS together and points facing to the right. Insert a third needle into the first stitch on each needle and knit these stitches together *(Fig. 1)*. * Insert the needle into the next stitch on each needle and knit these stitches together. Pass first stitch on right-hand needle over the second stitch and off the end of the needle. Repeat from * to end, knitting the pieces together and binding off as you go.

Fig. 1

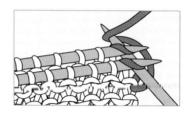

SKILL LEVELS

■□□□ BEGINNER	Projects for first-time knitters using basic knit and purl stitches. Minimal shaping.
■■□□ EASY	Projects using basic stitches, repetitive stitch patterns, simple color changes, and simple shaping and finishing.
■■■□ INTERMEDIATE	Projects with a variety of stitches, such as basic cables and lace, simple intarsia, double-pointed needles and knitting in the round needle techniques, mid-level shaping and finishing.
■■■■ EXPERIENCED	Projects using advanced techniques and stitches, such as short rows, fair isle, more intricate intarsia, cables, lace patterns, and numerous color changes.

YARN WEIGHTS

Yarn Weight Symbol & Names	LACE 0	SUPER FINE 1	FINE 2	LIGHT 3	MEDIUM 4	BULKY 5	SUPER BULKY 6
Type of Yarns in Category	Fingering, size 10 crochet thread	Sock, Fingering, Baby	Sport, Baby	DK, Light Worsted	Worsted, Afghan, Aran	Chunky, Craft, Rug	Bulky, Roving
Knit Gauge Range* in Stockinette St to 4" (10 cm)	33-40** sts	27-32 sts	23-26 sts	21-24 sts	16-20 sts	12-15 sts	6-11 sts
Advised Needle Size Range	000-1	1 to 3	3 to 5	5 to 7	7 to 9	9 to 11	11 and larger

*GUIDELINES ONLY: The chart above reflects the most commonly used gauges and needle sizes for specific yarn categories.

** Lace weight yarns are usually knitted on larger needles to create lacy openwork patterns. Accordingly, a gauge range is difficult to determine. Always follow the gauge stated in your pattern.

SATIN STITCH

Come up with needle at odd numbers and go down at even numbers (Fig. 2). Place stitches side by side, touching but not overlapping.

Fig. 2

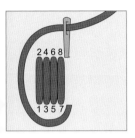

BACKSTITCH

Come up with needle at odd numbers and go down at even numbers (Fig. 3).

Fig. 3

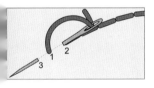

DUPLICATE STITCH

Duplicate Stitch is worked on Stockinette Stitch. Each knit stitch forms a V and you want to completely cover that V, so that the design appears to have been knit into the item. Each square on a chart represents one knit stitch that is to be covered by a Duplicate Stitch. Thread a yarn needle with an 18" (45.5 cm) length of yarn. Beginning at lower right of a design and with right side facing, bring the needle

up from the wrong side at the base of the V, leaving an end to be woven in later (never tie knots). The needle should always go between the strands of yarn. Follow the right side of the V up and insert the needle from right to left under the legs of the V immediately above it, keeping the yarn on top of the stitch (Fig. 4a), and draw through. Follow the left side of the V back down to the base and insert the needle back through the bottom of the same stitch where the first stitch began (Fig. 4b, Duplicate Stitch completed).

Continuing to follow chart, bring needle up through the next stitch. Repeat for each stitch, keeping tension even with tension of knit fabric to avoid puckering.

When a length of yarn is finished, run it under several stitches on back of work to secure.

Fig. 4a

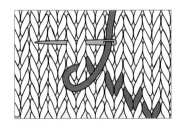

Fig. 4b

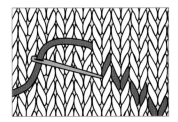

CROCHET SLIP STITCH

Begin with a slip knot on the hook. Insert hook as indicated in project instructions, yarn over and pull up a loop through stitch and loop on hook (Fig. 5). Repeat across. To finish, draw up a final loop and fasten off.

Fig. 5

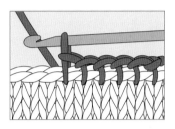

KNITTING NEEDLES		
UNITED STATES	ENGLISH U.K.	METRIC (mm)
0	13	2
1	12	2.25
2	11	2.75
3	10	3.25
4	9	3.5
5	8	3.75
6	7	4
7	6	4.5
8	5	5
9	4	5.5
10	3	6
10½	2	6.5
11	1	8
13	00	9
15	000	10
17	---	12.75
19	---	15
35	---	19
50	---	25

Yarn Information

The items in this leaflet were made using various weight yarns. Any brand of yarn may be used. It is best to refer to the yardage/meters when determining how many skeins to purchase. Remember, to arrive at the finished size, it is the GAUGE/TENSION that is important, not the brand of yarn.

For your convenience, listed below are the yarns used to create our photography models.

Baby Hat

Waverly for Bernat®

Cream Puff #55007

Celadon #55280

Leg Warmers

Waverly for Bernat®

Cream Puff #55007

Celadon #55280

Princess #55415

Ripple Stripe Blanket

Vanna's Choice®

Color A: Linen #099

Color B: Cranberry #180

Color C: Terra Cotta #124

Color D: Mustard #158

Color E: Fern #171

Teal Stripe Blanket

Patons® Canadiana

Pale Teal #10743

Medium Teal #10744

Winter White #10006

Hooded Sweater

Vanna's Choice®

Silver Blue #105

Vest

Red Heart® Super Saver®

Light Blue #381

Windsor Blue #380

Sweetie Toy

Vanna's Choice®

Color A: Taupe #125

Color B: Linen #099

Color C: Dusty Rose #140

Booties

Bernat™ Satin

Faded Glory Ombre #05433

Mitts

Green: Patons® Canadiana:

White #10005

Cherished Green #10230

Blue: Vanna's Choice®

White #100

Silver Blue #105

Fingerless Mitts

Vanna's Choice®

White #100

Dusty Rose #140

We have made every effort to ensure that these instructions are accurate and complete. We cannot, however, be responsible for human error, typographical mistakes, or variations in individual work.

Production Team: Produced for Leisure Arts, Inc. by Candice Jensen Productions – Editor: Heather Vantress – Layout: Rita Sowins – Technical editing: Sandi Rosner – Photography by: Liz Steketee; pages 10, 23, 24, 26, and 31 Silvana Di Franco